ዓላማ

A PURPOSE PURSUED
PASSIONATELY IS POWERFUL

DEBBIE ALAMREW

DEDICATION

This book is dedicated to my parents who sacrificed everything so I could live a life filled with opportunity. Abate (*my father*), thank you for being the greatest first love a girl could ever have by setting the most exemplary precedent of how to love through action, and for always pushing me to be the absolute best version of myself. Enate (*my mother*), thank you for loving me when I didn't love myself, and for instilling in me a Faith so powerful that fear no longer has a home in me. I am forever indebted to you both, and no words could ever express my gratitude. I pray that watching me walk in my purpose makes you proud.

TABLE OF CONTENTS

LEGACY   pg. 1

african girl
ode to ethiopia
holy land
victorious
sacrifice
alamrew
for the love of africa

LOVE   pg. 13

we all we got
when two become one
you took my breath away
too much and not enough
the hardest part of falling in love
learning to love
rainbow promise

LOSS   pg. 25

stolen moments
black lives matter too
heartbreak
moving on
heart wall
the greatest irony of love
black girl they crucify
neighborhood Nip
masterpiece

LIBERATION   pg. 41

fresh start
saved
your answers lie within you
i found me
finally free
woman
grace

LEGACY

Being of Ethiopian heritage and raised in Nigeria, I had the privilege of truly basking in African glory since birth. I wouldn't appreciate how much of an impact this had on me until I was a young adult. It played a pivotal role in shaping my identity and outlook on the world. I have always known the richness that lives in Africa, and I understood from an early age how the media portrays only that which they want you to know. As a child, I would tell my parents that I needed to share with the world what Africa was truly like. When we moved to London, I stayed true to this mission, and every school project I passionately completed in some way highlighted the beauty of Africa. I still walk in the same mission today and there is nothing that makes me prouder.

african girl

before i ever knew my mind
i felt my soul
drenched
in African pride.

ode to ethiopia

Ethiopian girl
Ethiopian girl

sitting on the floor clutching my grandmother's netela
hanging onto her every word
as her wisdom would flow
endlessly,
captivated by the beat
of the beads
on her rosary,
each one representing a prayer over my life
she covered me for the rest of my life
august 1st
the worst day of my life,
i carry her name with pride
a legacy that inspires me
to be half the woman she was
i aspire to be,

Ethiopian girl
Ethiopian girl

strength derived from my ancestors,
what we lack in wealth
as a nation
we countervail
in love, culture, and celebration
of a history so rich,
resilience in the face of adversity,
so many different ethnic groups
a beautiful rainbow of diversity
i, am Amara and Gondere
oh, Ethiopia hagere,

4

my parents native tongue
was how I first heard lullabies
and bedtime stories,
i fell in love with the rhythms,
words flowed like water
song-like and poetic,
i remember I wrote my first poem
in Amharic,

Ethiopian girl
Ethiopian girl

remember every summer you would get so excited
to fly back to the motherland
and explore the wonders of your heritage,
even before you were old enough to understand
just how sacred those trips were
your spirit was ignited,

as a teenager
those trips became more than just
playing games of gebeta with grandma
and dress up with your cousins
who would ooh and ahh
at all the latest fashions
you had brought over for them,
started to dig deeper
to discover your purpose,

Ethiopian girl
Ethiopian girl

a purpose pursued passionately is powerful,
while I will forever marvel
at the beauty of Ethiopia
my eyes are wide open
to how she needs the help of her children
there is nothing like a mother's love

Ethiopia,
ለአንቺ: ያለኝ: ፍቅር: የተለየ:ነው::
home is where the heart is
enate, no matter where life takes me
there is no doubt that home is you,
and everything that I do
is driven by what I can give back to
the place where my heart lies,

God please hear her prayers
as she cries
for her long lost children
who reside,
all around the world
in search of opportunity,
know that the unity
of sharing the same mother
is why,
every time I see another Ethiopian
i bow my head in respect
for I know that you will never neglect
our mother's love.

holy land

to be african is
my greatest privilege
for in her image
i see my lineage

her beauty unlike another
my eyes grow as i discover
the glory of my mother

scent of her morning rain
washes away remnants of pain
from a history they tried to steal
through her love is how we heal

the heat from her burning sun
ignites a fiery passion inside every one
of her children
who carry stories
about her glory
wherever they go

for the continent
is the heart of all mankind
and to know africa is to find
the heart of God.

victorious

my blood is victorious
it knows no defeat,
my ancestors sacrificed their lives
on battlefields
for Ethiopia to survive,

our independence they failed to steal
but can a country ever heal
from that type of horrific ordeal?

their attempts to colonize
an ongoing nightmare,
as they attack our minds
may they never forget
that we share
the same blood
and strength
as our ancestors,
so we too will fight
until victory.

sacrifice

O, the tales my father
would tell me,
to listen to him talk
with painful pride
about the country
that was once home,
i feel the sacrifices
of him and my mother
and the pressure
to go further.

alamrew

your name holds great significance
for in it a legacy is birthed
for better or for worse
that serves to define you

the name alamrew
crowned in honor
for my beloved grandfather
whom i never met
chose it for my father

in the ethiopian culture
the husband's first name
becomes the family name
creating his new legacy

so until the day i marry
with great pride i carry
the last choice of my grandfather.

for the love of africa

africa,
where my heart resides
bursting with pride
at the way she provides
for her tribe

the media paints an image
of corruption and poverty
but failure to portray us properly
results in your loss of discovery
a nation saturated in prosperity

our wealth so great
that westerners emulate
but our magic they will never consummate

the mother of all mankind
our rock, constantly undermined
praising you gives me peace of mind

the land of light
blazing bright
upon my soul,
in your earth our roots planted
magnificent fruits you bore
never taken for granted
midnight worship, for you we chanted

hear our prayers Lord
for the one whom we adore,

africa

LOVE

Love brings harmony and true joy. It can be an overwhelming rush of emotions that unexpectedly turns your entire world upside down. I lost myself trying to love. I poured into others love I didn't have to give and it left me feeling empty and vulnerable. I realized that the hate I had for myself was greater than any love I had inside of me. Learning to truly love myself has been immensely liberating as I let go of past guilt, shame, and regret. It has allowed me to experience all of the beautiful facets of love which have made my life so much more meaningful.

we all we got

i see you
Black Girl

a Queen to me
you will always be
see,
Black Girl Magic
is necessary
to conjure up the strength
to just exist sometimes,
when you cry
i cry sis,
'cause I know what it feels like to exist
in a country where we are the most
disrespected, unprotected, and neglected
individuals,

i see you
Black Girl

heart heavy from the pain of
the world's disdain,
shoulders weak from the weight
of the endless burdens you carry
while enduring their hate,
meant to make you break
but instead like Maya
still
you rise,

i see you
Black Girl

thank God you don't look like
what you've been through
skin, dark enough

to cover your scars
hips, wide enough
to birth a nation
you, beautiful Queen
reign supreme
don't you ever forget,

i see you
Black Girl.

when two become one

i gave my heart to you
you broke it in two
gave me back half
with half of yours too
told me put them together,
a whole comprised
of me and you
the truest love i ever knew.

19

you took my breath away

laying my head on your chest
my heart stopped
i caught my breath,
it began to beat again
but now our rhythms were the same.

too much and not enough

i loved you too much,
broke my back to heal your pain
spent my last dime to see you smile
neglected my loved ones
so you were never alone,
supported you to stand tall
you didn't care the cost was my downfall
put my future on the line
trying to build our future,

i loved you too much to lose you
but in the end i did,
because you didn't love me enough.

the hardest part of falling in love

i was afraid i would meet you,
the man of my dreams
fall head over heels
then you disappear,
now I'm stuck
living in my nightmare
where you never reappear.

learning to love

i wish that i could see myself
the way that you do,
if only i could glance through your eyes
then maybe i would realize
that i'm worthy of this love,

so easy it was for you
to see the best in me,
i couldn't comprehend
while i stand here holding
the broken pieces of me,
what you could see
in a defeated me,
every time you touched me
i battled to hide
the demons that lived inside,
you told me i was the most beautiful woman
in your eyes,
as your fingers traced my curves,
i longed to work up the nerve
to tell you why you shouldn't love me,

eventually you got tired
of telling me i was deserving,
loving me had drained you
with tears in your eyes you told me
that you could no longer go through
trying to make me love me,

it was then i understood,
until i loved myself i never would,
be capable of loving another.

rainbow promise

you were always beautiful
but you allowed the clouds
to dim your shine
now after all that crying
you, my darling
are the sun.

LOSS

The heart is truly the strongest muscle in the body, for as much as it breaks it still continues to beat. The loss of a loved one is undoubtedly one of the hardest experiences to make it through, and can often change the entire trajectory of your life. Relationships serve to teach you not only about the qualities of others, but also about who you are as a person. Some paramount lessons come from the relationships that don't work, and it is up to us to turn the heartache into healing. In order to heal, you must first allow yourself to feel the pain, and then you can begin to restore your broken heart.

stolen moments

i never really took the time
to think about
all of life's stolen moments,
and now the world
looks different,
sun no longer shines
as bright,
the birds now somber
have taken flight,
we are all in mourning
and forever will be
for the loss of you
still feels untrue,
you watered me for years
never got to see me blossom,
now all i can do is promise
though an endless flow of tears
to make you proud of me,
my eldest sister
Achi,
when you left
you took a part of me,
though you are now free
there isn't anything i wouldn't do
to get those stolen moments
back for us to see.

In loving memory of my beautiful sister, Acham Alamrew

29

black lives matter too

Black Lives Matter too,
and that too is for those of you
who seem to be placing an only in front of our movement
when in actuality
we, are about inclusion not exclusion
you see,
until all of us are free
then none of us truly can be,

i spent my early years living in the motherland
drowning in the pride of my ancestry,
at the age of three
i was reciting the history
of kings and queens who looked like me,
then I moved to the great USA
the land of the brave
and the home of the free,
but this freedom,
this freedom is conditional
and we are conditioned
to accept it without a fight,

the blacker the berry the sweeter the juice
the blacker the berry the tighter the noose,

slavery was abolished in 1865
but the thought of black people being free
further fueled the fire of white supremacy
and so the fight continued,
Harriet Tubman, Sojourner Truth, Rosa Parks,
Martin Luther King Jr., Malcolm X, Frederick Douglass,
Black Lives Matter,
their lives mattered,

as this new generation rises up
bearing the scars of slavery,
we stand on the shoulders of giants
and continue to fight to be free,
yet you can't understand why
you don't feel the same hurt that comes
with each new hash tag
as we are forced to witness another brother,
another sister
slain at the hands of those sworn
to protect and serve,
you can't understand how it feels
to be failed by an entire system
that sees so little value in our lives
it fails to hold anyone accountable,

justice has become a mere fantasy
as we weep in our unjust reality,
tears streaming down my face
as my eyes witness yet another execution
i sit here with my mouth open wide
speechless,
not because I have nothing to say
but because it feels as though
everything I say falls upon deaf ears,
please,
take a walk in my skin
the one with all this beautiful melanin,
so you can understand
how it feels to know,
that because of my complexion
i'm not worthy of the same protection,

you ask why we gather in protest
why we petition for change
why we march in the streets
screaming "BLACK LIVES MATTER!"
because as long as I can breathe

i will use my voice
to fight for the Eric Garner's
who can't breathe,

Trayvon Martin. Yvette Smith. Michael Brown.
Kisha Michael. Philando Castile. Wakiesha Wilson.
Tamir Rice. Sandra Bland. Alton Sterling.
Jimmy Atchison. Jemel Roberson. Botham Shem Jean.
Antwon Rose Jr., Rekia Boyd, Jonathan Ferrell.
Mya Hall, Jordan Baker, Miriam Carey.

the list goes on.

their lives matter.

heartbreak

can a broken heart ever heal again?
will it even beat the same?
and if it does
oh what a shame
for living with this pain
surely it will only break again.

moving on

a lost love
must be mourned,
do not allow another love in
until the last love has left your heart,
allow time to grow apart
but be warned
there is a chance
your heart will never dance
again.

heart wall

my gravest mistake
believing your love was safe,
you knocked down the wall
around my heart
only to rebuild a fortress
i fear can never be taken apart.

the greatest irony of love

loving the right person at the wrong time
having the wrong person when the time is right
the heart is the center of the body
but it beats on the left
maybe that's the reason the heart is not always right,
finding out that you love someone
right after they walk out of your life,
or thinking that you're over him
until he touches you
the sweetest sin,
your skin on my skin,
as your fingers trace my body
and you write poems inside me
that make me scream
in angst
for i know that after tonight
i will only feel you in my dreams.

black girl they crucify

Black girl cry
tears fall
in silence
unheard,

Black girl why
our screams drowned out
by the judgment
as our words fall on deaf ears
body paralyzed by fear,

Black girl shy
as they salivate at our curves
this pain we don't deserve
we suffer in darkness
our truth deserves the light,

Black girl dry
your eyes and stand up tall
our strength used against us
so when we fall
instead of compassion
we are accused
insulted and
abused,

Black girl fly
your wings deserve to soar high
remember who your ancestors are
for that is the strength you signify.

neighborhood Nip

a hood legend
habesha royalty
negus Nipsey
you left a legacy
beyond inspiring
ignited a fire in
every man and woman of color
daring us to desire
to be better,

you walked with such pride
in your Eritrean roots,
i hope you know all the Habesha kids you inspired
to walk in our skin and own our truth,
Ermias,
God will rise
now you're flying high,
served your purpose down here
left us in your Jesus year
a sacred transition
for a man on a Godly mission,

you taught us all about generational wealth
focused our attention on Dr. Sebi who was teaching health
listening to you makes me want better for myself,
a true leader in every sense of the word
you practiced what you preached with intention
they're calling you the Tupac of this generation,
that doesn't even give you the credit you deserve
can't stomach that this coward had the nerve,

you were so much greater than this place,
you knew life was more than just a sprint
it's a marathon
reached the upper echelon
damn I can't believe you're gone,

38

ran your victory lap
now you're passing the baton,
to what I pray is a generation
who grows from your inspiration,

hussle and motivate
that's the new anthem
this loss is more than I can fathom,
the highest human act is to inspire,
those were your words
you've set our souls on fire,

we will keep your spirit alive forever
take care of our own and live better,
your death will not be in vain
despite this overwhelming pain
you've left us in the body but your spirit's still alive
i vow to do my part for your all your messages to thrive,

man, I haven't stopped crying since Sunday
'cause I always knew that one day
i would have the opportunity
to thank you for all you did for the community,
this nightmare is beyond horrific
but what you left us with is prolific
your whole essence was prophetic.

In memory of Ermias Joseph Asghedom aka Nipsey Hussle
(August 15, 1985 - March 31, 2019).

masterpiece

her pain is colorful
artistic strokes of heartbreak
a portrait of betrayal
beautifully broken,
her textured timidness
an influence for intimidation,
the shape of her spirit
saturated to distortion
her canvas now unrecognizable
as spectators admire her scars
from afar,
abstract art
they call her.

LIBERATION

You cannot live with both Faith and fear existing inside you simultaneously. To have Faith is to trust God completely through the darkness. It took me a while to truly grasp that. Knowing that you were created in His image and placed on this earth to complete your purpose, is to know that God created you for a reason. If that doesn't make you feel exceptionally significant then I don't know what will. It is imperative to know who you are and not allow yourself to be molded by negative societal and familial influences. Stand firm in your beliefs, know what you deserve and don't settle for anything less. The purpose God placed on your heart and the talents that he blessed you with are His gifts to you. What you do with them are your gifts back to Him.

fresh start

run from that which broke you
leave behind all the heartache too
for despite what he said is true
you deserve to start anew.

saved

drowning in my insecurities
suffocated by my fears
burning in my self-hatred
deafened by my doubts
weeping through my lack of self-worth
blinded by my darkness
burdened by each breath I take,

i am a failure
but my God isn't.

your answers lie within you

comparing myself to others
trapped me within their boundaries
failing to see my true potential
i was searching for myself
in all the wrong places.

i found me

beautiful skin
filled with blemishes
representing every healed and unhealed wound
and even the unhealed will heal soon
every song I sing will be in tune,
every scripture I read will make me feel right
because I'm standing on God's promises
so I'm wrapped up tight,
with words as my weapon
i will fight a good fight,
my pen is my sword
the Word is my shield
i might get knocked down
but even in my darkness
by Him I am healed,
i overcame low self esteem
through my higher power I have been redeemed,
gone are my days of no self-worth
because God above placed me on this earth,
i will not be degraded, exploited, saturated with self-hatred
i will be loved, cherished and elevated
my birthday deserves to be celebrated,
i will not be manipulated, insulted or used
took a stand and refused to be abused,
found the master key to my identity
finally living in serenity.

finally free

i am now free
because i can finally see
you weren't good enough for me,

remember when you told me i wouldn't amount to anything,
you lied to my face and said i was your everything
instead you took my everything,
gave you all the love i had
leaving nothing for myself,

your hate for me flowed like an ocean,
drowning me with criticisms
suffocating me with jealousy
your words burned on my body
turning it into thick skin,

every morning i would wake up
wishing that i hadn't,
i tried to pray my way out
but by then self doubt had become my religion,

your love almost killed me
i knew this wasn't God's plan for me
but i had to get out in order to see,
if only you could now see
who i turned out to be.

woman

i am always in awe
at the strength of a woman
sacrificing herself
to nourish the universe
a woman's love
breathes life in the womb
her sanctified nature
to nurture
tasting her sweet nectar,
a privilege you don't deserve.

grace

my spirit had broke
as i lay in the bed
death i spoke
over my life,

this pain i couldn't mend
just praying for the end,
but my savior died
so i may live
sins set aside
my life is His,

tears stream down my face
as i reflect upon His grace,
the mercy He has shown me
i am so unworthy
from myself He saved me,

in my silent moments
is when I feel Him closest,
on Him i place my burdens
one thing i know for certain,
it is my faith that carries me
and finding God
that set me free.

If you would like to learn more about Debbie Alamrew and her work, please visit:

www.debbiethewriter.com

or you can send an email to:

info@debbiethewriter.com

ACKNOWLEDGMENTS

If you are reading this then that means I really did it, I published my poetry!! I am so filled with gratitude that you took the time to read my words and allowed me to share my heart with you. THANK YOU! I have been writing for as long as I can remember, and publishing my poetry has long been a dream of mine. Writing this book was harder than I thought it would be, yet much more rewarding than I could have ever anticipated.

I owe everything to my parents, Wolde and Aster Alamrew, who like so many immigrants made endless sacrifices for their children to be afforded greater opportunities than they were. Thank you for your selfless hearts. I am constantly in awe of the courage that you both possess, and I am privileged to be the daughter of a real King and Queen.

My best friend Jessica Williams, a very special thank you for your unwavering love and support. Your joy when I told you I was going to pursue this project, followed by your encouragement when the idea of completion seemed unmanageable, truly means the world to me. Also, thank you for designing and creating the beautiful cover for this book!

To my niece Ella, your birth has been the greatest gift and I am beyond honored to be your aunt. Watching you grow up has been such a beautiful blessing. I have always admired how you walk to the beat of your own drum and I pray that you never lose that. Thank you for being one of my greatest inspirations.

To my family and friends, you are my heart beat. You keep me inspired and filled with joy. Thank you for all the memories I will eternally hold close to my heart. I treasure each and every one of you with every fiber of my being. I love you.

Thank you to all the people I have encountered throughout my journey of life. I am a person who feels everything deeply and if you have ever been a part of my life then you have left some imprint on my heart. Some memories I relive with smiles while others bring painful tears to my eyes. I am grateful for all of them as they are what inspired the words on these pages.

Lastly, and most importantly, I give all the praise and glory to God. His grace is incredibly humbling and as undeserving of it as I may feel at times, I know that I am worthy because I am His child. My path has not been easy but I believe that every encounter and circumstance has been a part of His greater plan. I am grateful for purpose.

ABOUT THE AUTHOR

Debbie Alamrew is a poet, writer and spoken word performer of Ethiopian descent. She has been writing poetry since the tender age of nine and it was through her words that she discovered the power of her voice.

Debbie was born in London and spent her childhood living between England and Nigeria, spending every summer vacation in Ethiopia. At an early age she was exposed to different cultures and lifestyles which played an integral part in shaping her worldview. She credits her ability to relate so strongly with people from all walks of life to her unique upbringing.

In high school is where she began to develop and nurture her performance abilities as she excelled at LAMDA (London Academy of Music & Dramatic Art) and attended the Sylvia Young Theatre School, where notable alumni include Amy Winehouse, Emma Bunton, Leona Lewis and many more.

A graduate of the University of North Texas and recipient of a Juris Doctor from the University of Maine School of Law, it was while Debbie was a sophomore in college that she first found herself on stage performing spoken word. That was when her true passion was ignited. She has been performing since then on stages around the country, and the reactions she receives from people who are inspired, touched, and empowered are assurances that she is walking in her purpose.

Purpose is her debut poetry book in which she explores the four themes of legacy, love, loss and liberation which have been most dominant in her life. She writes from her heart and embraces her vulnerability as her greatest strength. A quality commonly viewed as weak, she has learned that vulnerability is the most authentic state to live in. There is a distinct strength in walking in your truth and she is driven by the passionate pursuit of her purpose.

Made in the USA
Coppell, TX
11 May 2020